# THE SECOND FLOOD

# THE SECOND FLOOD

## THE DISCIPLINE OF WORSHIP

*by*

## JOHN W. STEVENSON

**Destiny Image Publishers**
**P.O. Box 351**
**Shippensburg, PA 17257**

**"Speaking to the Purposes of God for this Generation"**

ISBN 1-56043-057-5

For Worldwide Distribution
Printed in the U.S.A.

# Acknowledgment

I would like to thank everyone who gave his support and encouragement during the writing of this book. I especially want to thank my pastor and friend, LaFayette Scales, for being an example of a true man of God, and all the family at Rhema Christian Center. My thanks to Annette McGee for helping put this all together. Thank you for all the hours spent editing and the little things you added. To Charlene Snowden and Widow's Mite International Ministries, thank you for believing in the gifts God has given me and the call on my life. Together we will touch the world with the gospel. I appreciate Kent Henry for sharing with me the importance of leading a disciplined life. The staff of H.I.M. Inc. has shared the vision with me, for which I am grateful; and a special thanks to Linda Jones. I would like to thank Don Nori and the staff at Destiny Image for their hard work and help in making this book a reality.

# Dedication

This book is dedicated to my wonderful wife Marissa, who is God's gift to me; to my children Gregory, Leslie, Nicholas, David and Christopher, who are the joys of my life; and to my mother, Patricia Stevenson, for always being there.

# Contents

# Contents

# Introduction

To the degree that you are willing to discipline your life, God will be able to accomplish His desired plan for you. It is to that degree of discipline that God is going to be able to accomplish in your life that which He has shown you, to bring to pass those desires that He has placed in your heart, and to bring about those things for which you are believing Him. It doesn't happen merely because God said it was going to happen. A lot depends upon you and me.

There are certain things in our lives that God will not override. He will not force us to do anything. I believe that when God shows us something about our lives, when He shows us the direction that He wants to take us or something that He wants to do, He is then looking for us to begin to align ourselves with where He wants to take us, based on that rhema word which we have received from Him. It is not totally our responsibility, but a great part of it is. For that reason, there are many today to whom God has spoken. He might have spoken to you, showing you things about your life about where He is going to take you and things that He will do in your life. You might be asking yourself, "Why isn't it happening? Why aren't these things taking place?" The Lord had to bring understanding to me concerning my own life. I had seen many things in the spirit pertaining to what God will do in my life. But when I looked at the things which He had accomplished in my life until that point, I immediately had one clear thought: He had not even begun to do what He had shown me He wanted to do. Then I had to ask myself, "Well, what is wrong? Is it that God is slothful?" No! That is not true. The fact is that there were certain things that I had not yet come to understand or walk in. There were certain things in my life that had yet to come together in order for the total picture to be what God wanted it to be. You might be in the same boat. But understand this: God is gracious and He is merciful. As you and I yield our lives, He will use us; yet He desires to do so much more. When you look at others' lives, and you see God using them in a great capacity, you need to realize that, more often than not, that person has disciplined his life to a level that allows God to work through him in many ways. So our goal, our task, our objective is to always strive to be more for Christ.

There is never a leveling-off point in Christ.

There is not a point of success in Him. Success is a process in life. God gives you a vision and He says, "I want to do this in your life." Then He helps you to accomplish it. But all the while you are reaching that goal, He is showing you something new. As we pass one test, one point, He takes us to the next thing He has for us to do. He wants to take us from glory to glory (II Cor. 3:18). This can only be accomplished by practicing a level of discipline in our daily Christian walks.

There are many varied areas of our lives that we could address concerning discipline, but we will concentrate on "The Discipline of Worship." I believe as we address the area of worship, with God as its focus, we will be put in contact with Him. He can then help us become disciplined in all other areas of life.

# Chapter I

## True Worship
## Touches All

**M**any of us are familiar with the scripture found in John 4:23. But the hour cometh, and now is, when the true worshipers shall worship the Father in spirit and in truth: for the Father seeketh such to worship Him." There is no option. It does not say "...they that worship Him *should try to* worship Him in spirit and in truth," or "*occasionally* worship Him in spirit and in truth." The Word says we *must* worship Him in spirit and in truth. From the beginning, when God created man, and even from before Adam's sin, God was continually wanting to fellowship with man and draw him to Himself. We read in Genesis that He came walking in the garden in the cool of the day looking for Adam. At that time Adam and Eve had already sinned and so they were hiding...

*And they heard the voice of the Lord God walking in the garden in the cool of the day: and Adam and his wife hid themselves from the presence of the Lord God amongst the trees of the garden. And the Lord God called unto Adam, and said unto him, Where art thou? And he said I heard thy voice in the garden, and I was afraid, because I was naked; and I hid myself.*

Genesis 3:8-10

God is continually trying to draw us to Him. In this day and age it is through the move of praise and worship that we are able to enter into that intimate place with God. For you and me to experience the shekinah glory of God, the glory or the radiance of God dwelling in the midst of His people, worship for us must be a lifestyle! Jesus said that they who worship the Father must do so in spirit and in truth. Part of that truth lies in allowing the way we live and what we say to match what we do and say when we are aware of His presence. It is only as we walk in obedience to His Word that we are able to worship in truth. Anything less is deception and a lie. Disobedience is a sin, and sin separates us from God! We must not allow ourselves to be deceived.

Psalm 138:1 says, "I will praise thee with my whole heart: before the gods will I sing praise unto thee." God desires that we worship Him with our whole heart. If we are going to worship in spirit and in truth, we must be honest about what is in our heart. We cannot truly worship God if we harbor any anger, bitterness, resentment, envy, hatred or any other sinful attitude against a brother or a sister. He sees it even when we hide it from one another. First John 4:20 says, "If a man says, I love God, and hateth his brother, he is a liar: for he that loveth not his brother whom he hath seen, how can he love God whom he hath not seen?" This tells us that if we are going to live our lives as worshipers, we must first be willing to love our brothers and sisters. All God requires is that we be honest both with ourselves and with Him. We read in First John 1:5-10, *"This then is the message which we have heard of him, and declare unto you, that God is light, and in him is no darkness at all. If we say that we have fellowship with him, and walk in darkness, we lie, and do not the truth: But if we walk in the light, as he is in the light, we have fellowship one with another, and the blood of Jesus Christ His Son cleanseth us from all sin. If we say that we have no sin, we deceive ourselves, and the truth is not in us. If we confess our sins, he is faithful and just to forgive us our sins, and to cleanse us from all unrighteousness. If we say that we have not sinned, we make him a liar, and his word is not in us.*" He tells us that if we simply confess, He will forgive us and cleanse us! If we do not confess, we will be judged.

Joshua Chapter seven teaches a lesson concerning hidden sin. We may hide things from one another, but God sees all things. Achan had stolen several articles as spoil when the sons of Israel conquered Jericho — something the Lord had prohibited. Because of his hidden sin, the men of Israel were defeated when they went up to fight against the small city of Ai. When the Lord was consulted, Achan's sin was revealed, and a Israelite stoned him to death at God's command.

Even as God dealt severely with Achan, so is He requiring us to deal with sin in our own lives. We must be honest with ourselves, not deceiving ourselves into thinking we can hide anything from God. If you and I are going to experience the glory and the anointing of God in our midst and in our homes, worship for us must be in every breath we take. As we recognize and begin to walk in this manner, then when we come in contact with people they will be blessed and we will have the effect in touching their lives that we read of in Luke 24:13-35:

*And, behold, two of them went that same day to a village called Emmaus, which was from Jerusalem about threescore furlongs. And they talked together of all these things which had happened. And it came to pass, that, while they communed together and reasoned, Jesus himself drew near, and went with them. But their eyes were holden that they should not know Him. And He said unto them, What manner of communications are these that ye have one to another, as ye walk, and are sad? And the one of them, whose name was Cleopas, answering said unto Him, Art thou only a stranger in Jerusalem, and hast not known the things which are come to pass there in these days? And He said unto them, What things? And they said unto Him, Concerning Jesus of Nazareth, which was a prophet mighty in deed and word before God and all the people: And how the chief priests and our rulers delivered him to be condemned to death, and have crucified him. But we trusted that it had been he which should have redeemed Israel: and beside all this, today is the third day since these things were done. Yea, and certain women also of our company made us astonished, which were early at the sepulchre; And when they found not his body, they came, saying, that they had also seen a vision of angels, which said that he was alive. And certain of them which were with us went to the sepulchre, and found it even so as the women had said: but him they saw not. Then he said unto them, O fools, and slow of heart to believe all that the prophets have spoken: Ought not Christ to have suffered these things, and to enter into his glory? And beginning at Moses and all the prophets, he expounded unto them in all the scriptures the things concerning himself. And they drew nigh unto the village, whither they went: and he made as though he would have gone further. But they constrained him, saying, Abide with us: for it is toward evening, and the day is far spent. And He went in to tarry with them. And it came to pass, as he sat at meat with them, he took bread, and blessed it, and brake, and gave to them. And their eyes were opened, and they knew him; and he vanished out of their sight. And they said one to another, Did not our heart burn within us, while he talked with us by the way, and while he opened to us the scriptures? And they rose up the same hour, and returned to Jerusalem, and found the eleven gathered together, and them that were with them, Saying, The Lord is risen indeed, and hath appeared to Simon. And they told what things were done in the way, and how he was known of them in breaking of bread.*

After Jesus had risen from the dead, He joined a couple of fellows as they were walking along. He asked them what was wrong, and they responded said that they had believed in this man Jesus and that now He was gone. They were hopeless. He spoke to them, saying, "You really do not understand what has happened. You do not believe." And the Bible says He began to share with them from the time of Moses and expounded on all the Scriptures concerning Himself. When He departed, they said, "Did not our hearts burn? This was from the words that He spoke, for His words were life to all who heard them.

When worship becomes a lifestyle, as you come come in contact with people your very conversation (and I am not speaking of necessarily quoting the Word of God verbatim, but of your very presence and conversation) will cause a burning and an illumination in the company of those you are with. Have you ever talked with someone, and although there was no deep involved conversation, you went away thinking, "That was a blessed conversation. I really enjoyed talking to that person. He really blessed me. He did not say anything very profound, but there was just something about his spirit." Have you ever experienced that? I have! And I have found that, more often than not, it is someone who has the type of relationship with God that is so ongoing that His anointing flows out of the conversation. You see, when worship is a lifestyle, then at some point in every conversation God begins to start talking. It is as though you give way to God and let Him have an opportunity to speak. All of a sudden you know you are saying something that is not even you. Your words become life. And the person listening to you is so blessed that he walks away from you and says, "Oh, my heart burns from that conversation." You walk away with tears in your eyes and say, "Oh, Jesus! Lord, that was You." You see, in the midst of the conversation, you are being blessed by what you are saying. "The liberal soul shall be made fat: and he that watereth shall be watered also himself" (Prov. 11:25). First Peter

4:11 instructs us to speak as the oracles of God. "If any man speak, let him speak as the oracles of God; if any man minister, let him do it as of the ability which God giveth: that God in all things may be glorified through Jesus Christ, to whom be praise and dominion for ever and ever. Amen." True worship will produce this result.

# Chapter II

## All Worship Belongs to God

**T**he object of our worship is God and God alone. You are probably saying, "I know that." But do you *really* know that? You see, what I have found is that, if I am not careful, there are times when my focus does not stay on God in worship, but it gets side-tracked. We are living in a society that makes heroes and stars out of just about everything and everybody, from sports professionals to rock music stars, talk show hosts, dogs, turtles, aliens, and even people in the ministry. It is easy for us to lift people up and to focus our attention and affection on them if we are not careful. That is why Proverbs 4:20-27 exhorts us:

*...My son, attend to my words; incline thine ear unto my sayings. Let them not depart from thine eyes; keep them in the midst of thine heart. For they are life unto those that find them, and health to all their flesh. Keep thy heart with all diligence; for out of it are the issues of life. Put away from thee a froward mouth, and perverse lips put far*

*from thee. Let thine eyes look right on, and let thine eyelids look straight before thee. Ponder the path of thy feet, and let all thy ways be established. Turn not to the right hand nor to the left: remove thy foot from evil.*

Throughout our Christian life there are times when God requires us to pull down pictures and idols in our life and past. He told Moses this in the plains of Moab.

*And the Lord spake unto Moses in the plains of Moab by Jordan near Jericho, saying, Speak unto the children of Israel, and say unto them, When ye are passed over Jordan into the land of Canaan; Then ye shall drive out all the inhabitants of the land from before you, and destroy all their pictures, and destroy all their molten images, and quite pluck down all their high places: And ye shall dispossess the inhabitants of the land, and dwell therein: for I have given you the land to possess it. And ye shall divide the land by lot for an inheritance among your families: and to the more ye shall give the more inheritance, and to the fewer ye shall give the less inheritance: every man's inheritance shall be in the place where his lot falleth; according to the tribes of your fathers ye shall inherit. But if ye will not drive out the inhabitants of the land from before you; then it shall come to pass, that those which ye let remain of them shall be pricks in your eyes, and thorns in your sides, and shall vex you in the land wherein ye dwell. Moreover it shall come to pass, that I shall do unto you, as I thought to do unto them.*

Numbers 33:50-56

As you can see, there were very specific instructions and, if the sons of Israel did not obey them, their lives were going to be miserable. Take time right now to ask the Lord if there is anything in your life that He is requiring you to pull down or put down. Whatever the Lord shows you, do not hesitate to do it! It is important that we remove anything and everything from around us that would keep us from focusing on God and God alone. Jesus said in Matthew 4:10, "...Get thee hence, satan: for it is written, thou shalt worship the Lord thy God, and Him only shalt thou serve." Worshiping God is our number one priority, and true worship of God translates into true service to the Lord.

You might be familiar with the passage of Scripture describing Mary and Martha. Martha

was busy getting a meal ready and she wanted
Mary to get up from the feet of Jesus to help
her.

> *Now it came to pass, as they went, that he
> entered into a certain village: and a certain
> woman named Martha received him into her
> house. And she had a sister called Mary,
> which also sat at Jesus' feet, and heard his
> word. But Martha was cumbered about much
> serving, and came to him, and said, Lord,
> dost thou not care that my sister hath left
> me to serve alone? bid her therefore that
> she help me. And Jesus answered and said
> unto her, Martha, Martha, thou art careful
> and troubled about many things: But one
> thing is needful: and Mary hath chosen that
> good part, which shall not be taken away
> from her.*

Luke 10:38-42

Jesus implied that Mary was in the place that
Martha needed to be in. We must understand
something. Many times what happens is that
service takes the place of worship. Often we
think that in our serving (being busy like Martha
was) we are worshiping God. But that is not
always true. When you and I make worship our

first priority, it causes us to serve God out of a pure heart. It causes us to seek His heart and to say, "Lord, what can I do for You today?" It causes us to set aside our own feelings, our own concerns, the things that seem so important to us in order to get in touch with what God really wants to do in us and through us. You may be someone who works at home or has small children. Of course that means many duties and responsibilities. However, even in the midst of all those things, there are times when all God is wanting you to do is to sit down for a moment and have a time of worship, a time that allows Him to minister to you as you worship Him — a time where you cast the weight of your cares on Him because He cares for you, and you are refreshed because you have been in His presence.

The other point I want to make is this: When you are truly serving God out of a desire to please Him, you won't be concerned about whether someone else is doing his part. Martha was trying to impress the Lord through her fine hospitality. Her motive was not pure. Often times we look around wondering, "Why isn't this brother or that sister busy for God? Why does it always fall on me?" But this is false humility and borderline pride. Elijah almost made this mistake, but God assured him he was not the only faithful one left. God had reserved for Himself 7,000 Israelites who had not forsaken Him

*And he said, I have been very jealous for the Lord God of hosts: because the children of Israel have forsaken thy covenant, thrown down thine altars, and slain thy prophets with the sword; and I, even I only, am left; and they seek my life, to take it away. And the Lord said unto him, Go, return on thy way to the wilderness of Damascus: and when thou comest, anoint Hazael to be king over Syria: And Jehu the son of Nimshi shalt thou anoint to be king over Israel: and Elisha the son of Shaphat of Abelmeholah shalt thou anoint to be prophet in thy room. And it shall come to pass, that him that escapeth the sword of Hazael shall Jehu slay: and him that escapeth from the sword of Jehu shall Elisha slay. Yet I have left me seven thousand in Israel, all the knees which have not bowed unto Baal, and every mouth which hath not kissed him.*

I Kings 19:14-18

True worship produces a true desire to serve God in whatever way He sees fit. When He calls, we respond — not looking to see who is noticing or who else will help, but with joy that we are counted worthy to serve Him.

# Chapter III

## Remember the Way to God's Heart

*A*fterward he brought me to the gate, even the gate that looketh toward the east: And, behold, the glory of the God of Israel came from the way of the east: and his voice was like a noise of many waters: and the earth shined with his glory. And it was according to the appearance of the vision which I saw, even according to the vision that I saw when I came to destroy the city: and the visions were like the vision that I saw by the river Chebar; and I fell upon my face. And the glory of the Lord came into the house by the way of the gate whose prospect is toward the east. So the spirit took me up, and brought me into the inner court; and, behold, the glory of the Lord filled the house.*

Ezekiel 43:1-5

When you and I understand the discipline of worship and when we understand worship as a lifestyle, when we assemble ourselves together in corporate worship the degree and magnitude of worship will enter into new levels that we have yet to experience. Many have been in great worship services. However, based on what I have seen in the spirit and what God has revealed to me in His Word, I believe we have not begun to touch the threshold of what God wants to do. As we continue to read, we see a glimpse of what it is that God wants to do. Ezekiel 43:2 says, "And, behold, the glory of the God of Israel came from the way of the east: and his voice was like a noise of many waters..." When you and I come together in corporate worship, there is a gathering together and a welling up in worship because of the lifestyles that we are living as worshippers. And whether we open up the windows of our churches or not, the greatness of the praise should sound like many waters to those that would be walking and traveling in the area. The Scriptures tell us that out of our bellies shall flow rivers of *living* waters! There should be a sense of excitement that causes people to know that there is something different here.

We need to understand that worship in God's presence must be pure. We read in Psalm 24:3-4 "Who shall ascend into the hill of the Lord? or who shall stand in his holy place? He that hath clean hands, and a pure heart; who hath not lifted up his soul unto vanity, nor sworn deceitfully." Worship in God's presence must be pure. Ezekiel 44:1,2,5 further explains this truth:

*Then he brought me back the way of the gate of the outward sanctuary which looketh toward the east: and it was shut. Then said the Lord unto me; This gate shall be shut, it shall not be opened, and no man shall enter in by it; because the Lord, the God of Israel, hath entered in by it, therefore it shall be shut. And the Lord said unto me, Son of man, mark well, and behold with thine eyes, and hear with thine ears all that I say unto thee concerning all the ordinances of the house of the Lord, and all the laws thereof; and mark well the entering in of the house, with every going forth of the sanctuary.*

Let me explain something here. When God moves in a miraculous way, there is a move into prophetic worship, or you are in private time with the Lord and you sense the manifest presence of God, you need to mark it. You need to make note of it. You need to have a sense and understanding of what is taking place at that very moment. This is the discipline of worship. Many times the Lord wants to show us something, impart something to us, or cause us to enter a place of intimacy we have not experienced before, but we don't know how to get there. He says, "Son of man, mark well, and behold with thine eyes, and hear with thine ears all that I say unto thee concerning all the ordinances of the house of the Lord..." For a long time when a thought or an idea would come to me concerning a song or a message, I would say, "Oh, I'll get around to working on it later." The next thing I knew, it was gone. So I would try to bring it back again, but it just wouldn't quite be the same. But then I started to listen. When the Lord began to impart a song to me, wherever I was, I would sing it over and over. If it was a word or thought, I would repeat it out loud. Sometimes I would be in my car or on my job and I could not stop to take the time to really hear the Lord. Then I would say, "Holy Spirit, I commit this unto You right now. And when I get to the place where I can work on it, I trust that You will bring it back to my remembrance." I had faith to do this because John 14:26 says, "But the Comforter, which is the Holy Ghost, whom the Father will send in my name, he shall teach you all things, and bring all things to your remembrance, whatsoever I have said unto you." This is part of the discipline of worship. There

are times when you and I in a corporate setting
enter into a place of worship and need to understand why we are there or how we got there.
"Mark well the entering of the house, with every
going forth of the sanctuary." There are certain
things that we should be doing in our personal
lives that help us to come together and know
with a "holy expectancy" that God is going to
move. When we talk about the discipline of worship, then we understand that there are certain
things that, if we will make note of them and
move on them, we will see that God will honor
later.

One example from my life is this: I had to get
to the place that I was going to be serious about
worshiping God. He told me that I needed to set
aside time; I now set aside the time to worship
like I do when I prepare to teach the Word of
God. You may say, "What can you do? Sit down
and sing a few songs?" Yes, that is just what I
do. I sit down and sing some songs and get into
the presence of God. You might say, "Well, I do
not sing." That's all right. Worship is not just
singing or music. It's giving praise and adoration
to something or someone. You can begin by speaking of God's loving kindness, His tender mercy,
His abundant grace, and other attributes.

It is in our private times with the Lord that He will tell us what He likes. As I play my instrument and sing to the Lord, I sense His anointing on certain chords and melodies that I play. I have played chords or simple melodies that have elevated our worship services: but I have usually played them before. I have played those chords the night before a service in my private time with God, even though I don't sing any words to them. But when we begin to discipline ourselves in worship, there are certain things that we will know are touching God's heart. He will say, "I like that." You will sense His presence. What I have done, and what you need to do, is to get to the place where when you recognize His anointing on a song or chorus you make a note of it. You see, because my wife knows which foods I like, she will make a special effort to make them. This is because she knows what I like and she wants to please me. It's the same way with the Father. When you understand what God likes, you make a note of it. So I know that in my time that I spend before the Lord that He will let me know exactly what ministers unto Him and what does not. I will play some songs and ask the Lord what He thinks about this one and that one. And then all of a sudden, I will begin to sense His anointing, His manifested presence, and I will make a note of whatever I am playing or singing at that time. When you understand the discipline of worship, then you will begin to make note of the things that you know bless God in your time with Him. When it is time to come together collectively, all you must do is remember. You might have been singing to the Lord earlier that day, "I love you, Lord. I magnify Your name." You felt His anointing on you, and you knew God was blessed by hearing you sing that to Him. And so, when we come together in corporate worship, and we begin to sing in the spirit and in open worship, all you have to do is remember your song. "I call to remembrance my song in the night: I commune with mine own heart: and my spirit made diligent search" (Ps. 77:6). Instead of trying to think of something to sing, or looking at other people, sing what you sang to Him when you were with Him earlier. God honors that.

So, we have to be sensitive enough to take notes — spiritual notes. As a worship leader and chief musician, many times I am in a service playing and I ask the Lord what He wants me to play next. No song comes to mind, and so I'll play a melody or chorus that I remember sensing His anointing on. You know what? It never fails,

God's anointing begins to flow. There are times when He will tell me to play certain chords or melodies and His anointing fills the room. Many times this type of worship releases an anointing for prophetic ministry to take place: "[Elisha said,] But now bring me a minstrel. And it came to pass, when the minstrel played, that the hand of the Lord came upon him. And he said, Thus saith the Lord..." (II Kings 3:15, 16a). I believe there should never be a time that we come together for worship that we don't end at a place where God can begin to move prophetically amongst His people. This is not just for worship leaders or musicians; God is wanting to move through His entire Body this way. We worship God wherever we are, whenever we can! It may be in a song. It may be through a word of praise. It may be with uplifted hands. It may be through tears of joy. We should come into a place in worship in which anything could happen. We get into His presence, then we can believe God for miracles. We need to get into His presence so that we are all standing in awe and wondering, "Lord, what are you going to do next?" He may say, "I am going to heal that lady in the back row who is having chest pains." Then He begins to move through the congregation ministering to His people.

I believe this is the way God wants to minister in our midst. I believe it is the new move of the Spirit coming upon us. In order for Him to do this, we must be willing to seek Him daily and to keep the charge. "Therefore thou shalt love the Lord thy God, and keep his charge, and his statutes, and his judgments, and his commandments, alway" (Deut. 11:1). "I beseech you brethren... (Matt. 12:1 and 2).

# Chapter IV

## A Charge
## We Have to Keep

*A*nd thou shalt say to the rebellious, even to the house of Israel, Thus saith the Lord God; O ye house of Israel, let it suffice you of all your abominations, in that ye have brought into my sanctuary strangers, uncircumcised in heart, and uncircumcised in flesh, to be in my sanctuary, to pollute it, even my house, when ye offer my bread, the fat and the blood, and they have broken my covenant because of all your abominations. And ye have not kept the charge of mine holy things: but ye have set keepers of my charge in my sanctuary for yourselves. Thus saith the Lord God; No stranger, uncircumcised in heart, nor uncircumcised in flesh, shall enter into my sanctuary, of any stranger that is among the children of Israel. And the Levites that are gone away far from me, when Israel went astray, which went astray away from me after their idols; they shall even bear their iniquity. Yet they shall be ministers in my sanctuary, having charge at *the gates of the house, and ministering to the house: they shall slay the burnt offering and the sacrifice for the people, and they shall stand before them to minister unto them. Because they ministered unto them before their idols, and caused the house of Israel to fall into iniquity; therefore have I lifted up mine hand against them, saith the Lord God, and they shall bear their iniquity. And they shall not come near unto me, to do the office of a priest unto me, nor to come near to any of my holy things, in the most holy place: but they shall bear their shame, and their abominations which they have committed. But I will make them keepers of the charge of the house, for all the service thereof, and for all that shall be done therein.*

*Ezekiel 44:6-14*

When I read this, the Lord said to me, "My people need to understand that you cannot try to live a life without worship, not living by the ordinances of the Word of God and then expect to turn around and enter into My presence every time or any time *you* feel like it." The sons of Israel began to do what they wanted to do and did not keep the charge He gave them. Many people today think they can live any way they want, but you need to understand that you cannot minister to the desires and the passions of the flesh Monday through Saturday and then turn around and try to minister to God on Sunday. What is the charge? The word "charge" in the Old Testament comes from the word mishmereth. It means "to watch; the act of custody; a guard, service, preservation, command, law." Deuteronomy 11:1 says, "Therefore thou shalt love the Lord thy God, and keep his charge, and his statutes, and his judgments, and his commandments, *alway*." Jesus gave His disciples a charge in John 15:10-17.

*If ye keep my commandments, ye shall abide in my love; even as I have kept my Father's commandments, and abide in his love. These things have I spoken unto you, that my joy might remain in you, and that your joy might be full. This is my commandment, That ye love one another, as I have loved you. Greater love hath no man than this, that a man lay down his life for his friends. Ye are my friends, if ye do whatsoever I command you. Henceforth I call you not servants; for the servant knoweth not what his lord doeth: but I have called you friends; for all things that I have heard of my Father I have made known unto you. Ye have not chosen me, but I have chosen you, and ordained you, that ye should go and bring forth fruit, and that your fruit should remain: that whatsoever ye shall ask of the Father in my name, He may give it you. These things I command you, that ye love one another.*

Romans 12:1,2 is a charge for us today.

*I beseech you therefore, brethren, by the mercies of God, that ye present your bodies a living sacrifice, holy, acceptable unto God, which is your reasonable service. And be not conformed to this world: but be ye transformed by the renewing of your mind, that ye may prove what is that good, and acceptable, and perfect, will of God.*

Also consider the Book of Ephesians. It charges us concerning our relationship with one another and our position in Christ. It speaks of how God has blessed us — salvation from sin, our hope, God's plan, Christ's love, oneness in the Body of Christ, a new way of thinking, living a life of love, our relationship as husbands and wives, children, being servants, and standing in God's armor. I believe all of this is a part of the charge we have been given and must be kept. It takes a conscious decision to live holy. The Word of God is our charge!

When we talk about the discipline of worship, we must understand that there has to be a conscious decision in our mind that our life is wholly yielded to one ministry — and that is the ministry unto God. Levites were the ones appointed priests. But there were three classifications of Levites. The first group we find in Ezekiel 44:6. These were "The rebellious ones" and God said they would not have a place at all! They had become an abomination to God. They did not keep charge of His holy things (Ezekiel 44:8,9). They had moved to a place of rebellion, which is as the sin of witchcraft. "For rebellion is as the sin of witchcraft, and stubbornness is as iniquity and idolatry. Because thou hast rejected the word of the Lord, He hath also rejected thee from being king" (I Sam. 15:23). It is an abomination before God. Galatians 5:19-21 tells us that witchcraft is a work of the flesh. "Now the works of the flesh are manifest, which are these...witchcraft...of the which I tell you before, as I have also told you in time past, that they which do such things shall not inherit the kingdom of God." You see, the rebellious refuse to accept

God's Word and would rather lean on the arm of
the flesh (Ezek. 44:7). There are many today who
refuse to hear the Word of the Lord, or the Holy
Spirit. They would rather continue on in the
traditions of men and rely on the flesh. The end
result for them will be the same as it was for the
rebellious ones in Ezekiel. It was the same for
Saul: "Because thou hast rejected the word of
the Lord, he hath also rejected thee..." (I Sam.
15:23b)

The second classification of Levites may be
seen in Ezekiel 44:10-14.

*And the Levites that are gone away far from
me, when Israel went astray, which went
astray away from me after their idols; they
shall even bear their iniquity. Yet they shall
be ministers in my sanctuary, having charge
at the gates of the house, and ministering to
the house: they shall slay the burnt offering
and the sacrifice for the people, and they
shall stand before them to minister unto
them. Because they ministered unto them
before their idols, and caused the house of
Israel to fall into iniquity; therefore have I
lifted up mine hand against them, saith the
Lord God, and they shall bear their iniquity.*

*And they shall not come near unto me, to do the office of a priest unto me, nor to come near to any of my holy things, in the most holy place: but they shall bear their shame, and their abominations which they have committed. But I will make them keepers of the charge of the house, for all the service thereof, and for all that shall be done therein.*

These Levites also went astray but they were not the initiators. However, God said, "You followed after them, even though you knew the truth! For that reason you will only have charge at the gates of the house, ministering to the house and to the people, but you will not come near unto Me to do the office of a priest unto Me." In verse 13, we see that these Levites were not only prohibited from coming near to the Lord: "...nor to come near to any of my holy things, in the most holy place..." They were not allowed to enter into His presence because they did not keep the charge.

Many today are only worshiping from the outer court. There are some who are only ministering to the people, the congregation. This is not God's desire, nor is it His best for us. Jesus gave His life so that you and I could enter into the presence of the living God. We must be willing to discipline our lives as worshipers, and be determined to keep the charge.

I don't know about you, but I know that there was a time when I was not living a disciplined life as a worshiper. It is very easy to discern. You see around you people who are entering into the presence of God and you wonder why you are not. Have you ever been there? I am going to be honest with you, because that is the only way that we are going to affect each other's lives as Christians. We must be honest with one another, willing to be transparent. There have been some times in the past when I have stood up and led worship, and God moved mightily. I was blessed like everybody else. But afterwards I have gone down from the platform and cried because I knew that, had my life been more disciplined, we probably could have gone much further in our worship service. Where we go corporately is based on where we are individually. Every person plays some part! The degree to which you are willing to discipline your life is the degree to which God is able to accomplish that which He desires to do in you and through you! When it comes to praise and worship and that which you and I see and are believing God for, when we come together and we have disciplined our lives as worshipers, there will be nothing there to hinder the flow of God. There are some people who come into church who are not Christians. But do you know what? When believers come together and that anointing begins to flow, and the rivers begin to flow, it even affects them in the spirit. The anointing of God begins to flow. It is only in the presence of God that we change. It is only as we enter into God's face that we change.

These Levites were close, but they weren't close enough. You need to ask yourself how close you have really been. I know when I am in God's face and when I am at a distance. And being at a distance is not a good feeling. The Scriptures continue:

*"But the priests the Levites, the sons of Zadok [Zadok means "righteous"], that kept the charge of my sanctuary when the children of Israel went astray from me, they shall come near to me to minister unto me, and they shall stand before me to offer unto me the fat and the blood, saith the Lord God: They shall enter into my sanctuary, and they*

*shall come near to my table, to minister unto me, and they shall keep my charge.*
Ezekiel 44:15,16

This is where we want to be — because we have kept the charge, because we have kept the standard, because we have lived the disciplined life of a worshiper, we can enter into the presence of God unhindered.

Ezekiel 46:9 says, *"But when the people of the land shall come before the Lord in the solemn feasts, he that entereth in by the way of the north gate to worship shall go by the way of the south gate; and he that entereth by the way of the south gate shall go forth by the way of the north gate: he shall not return by the way of the gate whereby he came in, but shall go forth over against it."* When you enter into worship, you should never leave the same way you came. There should be something that has changed in your life. The Scriptures say we are changed from glory to glory. You cannot enter into the presence of God and leave the same way you came. Understand that. You may try, but you will either leave transformed by the power of God or you will leave convicted by the power of God. The place for you and me and the blessing is that we leave praising our God that we have been in His presence and that He has been with us.

# Chapter V

## Expect His Manifest Presence

**W**hen we come together we should have what is called a "holy expectancy." We should anticipate a great move of God. We say to ourselves, "Lord, I have been with You all week. I've been talking to You all week. I was worshiping You at work. I was talking to You when I was at home washing the dishes. I was worshiping You when I was sorting the laundry. I was worshiping You when I was cutting the grass. All week I have been worshiping You. And, Lord, I know because of the well and the river You have placed in me that when I get in corporate worship and I get with my brothers and sisters who have been worshiping You all week, too, we are going to be able to release rivers of praise." The Bible says that where two or three are gathered together in His Name, He is there! The Word says He inhabits the praises of His people. So when we come together there should be a holy expectancy that something is going to happen here. God is going to do something great. But it comes from that disciplined life of worship.

When you come together with the body and you don't know what is going to happen, it is because you haven't been worshiping God. One of the blessings for me is when I get before God and I spend time on my instrument or in prayer, and I spend that time in His face; I know what is going to happen. I know what is going to happen because I have already seen it in the spirit. He gives me a glimpse of it. I have a sense of it. And I know that when I come together with God's people, the service has got to explode. That is supposed to be our expectation. That is where we are supposed to be. We read in Exodus chapters 24-40, that Moses knew that when he entered into the tabernacle that he was entering into the presence of God. When we talk about the holy expectancy of God, we need to recognize that we are talking about coming together knowing that God is in our midst and that He is going to do something great. I am not talking about the cliche, "Something good is going to happen today," or some of the other nice sayings people have come up with. But I am saying that as we come together our prayer can be "Lord, I have been worshiping You all week and now as I enter into Your presence with the rest of the Body of Christ, I can believe for a great move of Your

Spirit. I can believe for miracles in this setting. I can believe for healings in this setting. I can believe to hear from You like I have never heard from You before because we are coming together." When we look at the early Church in Acts chapter four, we find that the people came together in praise and prayer expecting signs and wonders to be done.

*And when they heard that, they lifted up their voice to God with one accord, and said, Lord, thou art God, which hast made heaven, and earth, and the sea, and all that in them is: Who by the mouth of thy servant David hast said, Why did the heathen rage, and the people imagine vain things? The kings of the earth stood up, and the rulers were gathered together against the Lord, and against His Christ. For of a truth against thy holy child Jesus, whom thou hast anointed, both Herod, and Pontius Pilate, with the Gentiles, and the people of Israel, were gathered together, For to do whatsoever thy hand and thy counsel determined before to be done. And now, Lord, behold their threatenings: and grant unto thy servants, that with all boldness they may speak thy word, stretching forth thine hand to heal; and that signs and*

*wonders may be done by the name of thy
holy child Jesus. And when they had prayed,
the place was shaken where they were
assembled together; and they were all filled
with the Holy Ghost, and they spake the
word of God with boldness. And the multitude of them that believed were of one heart
and of one soul: neither said any of them
that aught of the things which he possessed
was his own; but they had all things common.
And with great power gave the apostles wit-
ness of the resurrection of the Lord Jesus:
and great grace was upon them all. Neither
was there any among them that lacked: for
as many as were possessors of lands or houses
sold them, and brought the prices of the
things that were sold, and laid them down at
the apostles' feet: and distribution was made
unto every man according as he had need.
And Joses, who by the apostles was sur-
named Barnabas, (which is, being inter-
preted, The son of consolation,) a Levite, and
of the country of Cyprus, having land, sold
it, and brought the money, and laid it at the
apostles' feet.*

**Acts 4:24-37**

In Acts chapter two, we find that these believers came together with that expectancy. On the day of Pentecost it says that there was the sound of a mighty, rushing wind. There was an expectancy because Jesus had said, "...tarry ye in the city of Jerusalem, until you be endued with power from on high." They were praying. They were fasting. They were saying, "Look, I don't know what is going to happen, but He told us to wait, and we are going to wait. We are going to get into agreement. We are going to wait. We are going to wait." Then all of a sudden, once they got into agreement, here it came. Once they got into agreement, it happened. There were so many supernatural acts in the early Church.

*But a certain man named Ananias, with Sapphira his wife, sold a possession, and kept back part of the price, his wife also being privy to it, and brought a certain part, and laid it at the apostles' feet. But Peter said, Ananias, why hath Satan filled thine heart to lie to the Holy Ghost, and to keep back part of the price of the land? Whiles it remained, was it not thine own? and after it was sold, was it not in thine own power? why hast thou conceived this thing in thine heart? thou hast not lied unto men, but unto God. And Ananias hearing these words fell down, and gave up the ghost: and great fear came on all them that heard these things. And the young men arose, wound him up, and carried him out, and buried him. And it was about the space of three hours after, when his wife, not knowing what was done, came in. And Peter answered unto her, Tell me whether ye sold the land for so much? And she said, Yea, for so much. Then Peter said unto her, How is it that ye have agreed together to tempt the Spirit of the Lord? behold, the feet of them which have buried thy husband are at the door, and shall carry thee out. Then fell she down straightway at his feet, and yielded up the ghost: and the young men came in, and found her dead, and, carrying her forth, buried her by her husband. And great fear came upon all the church, and upon as many as heard these things.*

Acts 5:1-11

The agreement of Ananias and Sapphira was strong enough to bind them into an unholy alliance which led to death. Acts 9:36-43 also gives an account of the miraculous.

*Now there was at Joppa a certain disciple named Tabitha, which by interpretation is called Dorcas: this woman was full of good works and almsdeeds which she did. And it came to pass in those days, that she was sick, and died: whom when they had washed, they laid her in an upper chamber. And forasmuch as Lydda was nigh to Joppa, and the disciples had heard that Peter was there, they sent unto him two men, desiring him that he would not delay to come to them. Then Peter arose and went with them. When he was come, they brought him into the upper chamber: and all the widows stood by him weeping, and shewing the coats and garments which Dorcas made, while she was with them. But Peter put them all forth, and kneeled down, and prayed; and turning him to the body said, Tabitha, arise. And she opened her eyes: and when she saw Peter, she sat up. And he gave her his hand, and lifted her up, and when he had called the saints and widows, presented her alive. And it was known throughout all Joppa; and many believed in the Lord. And it came to pass, that he tarried many days in Joppa with one Simon a tanner.*

Peter expected that coming into a position of agreement with the Word of God would be sufficient to raise Dorcas from the dead. In a further example, another was raised from the dead.

*And upon the first day of the week, when the disciples came together to break bread, Paul preached unto them, ready to depart on the morrow; and continued his speech until midnight. And there were many lights in the upper chamber, where they were gathered together. And there sat in a window a certain young man named Eutychus, being fallen into a deep sleep: and as Paul was long preaching, he sunk down with sleep, and fell down from the third loft, and was taken up dead. And Paul went down, and fell on him, and embracing him said, Trouble not yourselves; for his life is in him.*

Acts 20:7-10

The key here is that these people were in agreement and did not mind waiting on God. I believe the example that best fits our topic is found in Second Chronicles 5:11-14.

*And it came to pass, when the priests were come out of the holy place: (for all the priests that were present were sanctified, and did not then wait by course: Also the Levites which were the singers, all of them of Asaph, of Heman, of Jeduthun, with their sons and their brethren, being arrayed in white linen, having cymbals and psalteries and harps, stood at the east end of the altar, and with them an hundred and twenty priests sounding with trumpets:) It came even to pass, as the trumpeters and singers were as one, to make one sound to be heard in praising and thanking the Lord; and when they lifted up their voice with the trumpets and cymbals and instruments of music, and praised the Lord, saying, For he is good; for his mercy endureth for ever: that then the house was filled with a cloud, even the house of the Lord; So that the priests could not stand to minister by reason of the cloud: for the glory of the Lord had filled the house of God.*

When they came together "of one accord" and making "one sound," the glory of God was so great that the priests could not stand to minister. How do we cultivate a holy expectancy? By practicing the presence of God in our daily lives.

I did not know as I was growing up and became involved in music that my life would take this direction in praise and worship in terms of what God is doing today. But when I look back, I can see that God has always had a plan for my life, just as He does for yours. As we become sensitive to His voice, He will make that plan more clear.

# Chapter VI

## Practice
## the Presence
## of God

*And be not drunk with wine,
wherein is excess; but be filled
with the Spirit; Speaking to yourselves in psalms and hymns and spiritual
songs, singing and making melody in your
heart to the Lord; Giving thanks always for
all things unto God and the Father in the
name of our Lord Jesus Christ.*

You see, practicing His presence begins in our
daily walk. While living out the demands of the
day, we are filled with an inward worship and
adoration. In the course of each day you need to
begin to discipline yourself to make melody to
the Lord. Begin to make melody in your heart.
It doesn't just happen. *You* have to start it. One
day I realized, "Hey, I can write songs." On the
day that I spoke that to myself, I also purposed
in my heart that I was going to cultivate that
gift. I was going to use it. I was going to develop
it. I was going to make it into something that
would bring glory to God. I didn't know then
what I know now, but what I did was to discipline

myself to sing unto the Lord in the spirit, to make melody in my heart, to sing unto God no matter where, no matter when, no matter what the situation. You have to do the same thing. Maybe you do not play an instrument or sing. But you must say to yourself, "I am a worshiper." Seek God as to how He desires you to worship Him. Believe it or not, for some it will be through your job that you worship Him. Your work will be such an excellent testimony and example that your co-workers will speak well of your work long after you are gone.

> *Now there was at Joppa a certain disciple named Tabitha, which by interpretation is called Dorcas: this woman was full of good works and almsdeeds which she did. And it came to pass in those days, that she was sick, and died...and all the widows stood by him weeping, and showing the coats and gar-ments which Dorcas made, while she was with them.*
>
> Acts 9:36,37a, and 39b

Worship for many others may be through service at home and the care of what God has placed in your hands. Whatever it may be, purpose in your heart to do it with all your heart!

Let us look at Ephesians 6:18. "Praying always with all prayer and supplication in the Spirit, and watching thereunto with all perseverance and supplication for all saints." We have to get to the place, saints, where we are "practicing the presence of God." You see, if you practice His presence when you are by yourself, it is not so hard to sense the presence of God when you come together with other believers. As part of being a disciplined worshiper and a disciplined life of worship, we begin to practice the presence of God. Have you ever been out somewhere when you suddenly felt like praying in the spirit? Sometimes I am just walking along and all of a sudden the presence of God is there. It's just as real as if someone were walking next to me. Then I find myself praying in the spirit. That is practicing the presence of God. You may be driving along and suddenly notice the presence of God there and begin to worship Him. You begin to practice the presence of God. You may be at home sitting and watching TV, and you feel His presence is there. Turn off the TV. It takes *discipline*. Let's talk a little about television.

I think it goes without saying that TV is one of the primary tools of the enemy. And many people have cable TV and video tapes. When I was growing up, one of the things that I really enjoyed was watching movies. I liked to watch late movies, the scary ones. Today, because of the evil of the times, man's imagination has gotten worse. There are many programs out there now that will really leave you vexed in your spirit. I found that when I had cable TV, I used to like to watch movies. I would look for the good suspense movies and the thrillers. And then one day the Lord said to me, "Remember when you were little and you liked to stay up and watch movies?" There used to always be two movies, and it seemed like they always had the scariest one on second. By then I was going to bed by 2:00 sometimes 3:00 a.m. I found I had not changed this pattern. And I knew that I had to make a decision. I had to discipline myself to say, "I am not going to do that any more." Right now, I don't even have cable TV. And it's good that I don't, for now. Maybe later we'll get it so my children can watch some children's programs. You have to know where to draw the line. And then do it! There are certain things that God may be speaking to you right now. He is saying that you need to be disciplined in a certain area or let a certain thing go if you want to move into where the Levites, the sons of Zadok, were and come in and minister to Him unhindered. But it is a matter of setting aside the time to get into God's presence and to practice His presence. When you learn to practice His presence, you know God is there. You know when He is moving. And, because of that, when more than one of us comes with a holy expectancy, it changes the whole atmosphere of the room.

Now, let me talk with you about worship services. It is great to come and fellowship, but our primary objective when we come into a worship service should be to worship God and to minister unto Him. It is all right to greet one another when coming into the church and to praise the Lord and embrace, but when we come in the sanctuary, we should enter in with an expectancy. We should begin to enter in with an attitude of prayer and worship as to what God is going to do. Many times we come in and we are talking with one another about a lot of different things. Some may be talking about their job, or about their children or whatever. Then all of a sudden, when the worship leader says, "Praise the Lord," everyone stands up and says, "Hallelujah!" That is the reaction. But your spirit, your mind, and your heart is not ready to worship. And for that reason we have to sing one song and another song and another song and another song before we all get into the same flow and into an attitude of worship. Now, does that make sense to you?

We are to come in having lived our lives throughout the week as an heir of the kingdom, listening to the voice of God, and obeying His Word. When this is true, you know that when you enter into public worship you are going to hear from God because you have that expectancy. When we come in, our hearts should be set on the adoration of the King of Glory. We need to think about His majesty, His tenderness. We need to see Him high and lifted up, as we read in Isaiah chapter six where it says His train filled the temple. We need to see Him the way Isaiah saw Him when he said, "Woe is me!" When you come with that expectancy, God is going to meet you there.

When we come in, we need to begin to pray. We need to begin to lift up the pastor to the Lord. We need to begin to lift up the ministry staff and those who will be vital in the service for that setting. We need to be praying. Unless you have been in public ministry, you never really understand what the speaker is battling and how the enemy many times is trying to do things to subvert his attention and get him off track. When we come together through disciplined worship, and we are in a place where we are coming with that expectancy of what God is going to do, the enemy cannot get in through any means. Everything is blocked off. We need to set aside all of our inhibitions and focus on the Lord, being open for what He wants to do. You and I have to come to a place of understanding that as worshipers we have a vital part to play in every service.

# Chapter VII

## Release
## His Anointing

**W**e need to understand and recognize that in you and in me there is a stream. There is a river. And what you want when you enter a worship service is for that river to flow forth unhindered, unstopped by anything.

*There is a river, the streams whereof shall make glad the city of God, the holy place of the tabernacles of the Most High. God is in the midst of her; she shall not be moved: God shall help her, and that right early.*

Psalm 46:4, 5

You and I need to recognize that God has placed in us a pool of His anointing. Do you believe that? Let us read John 7:38-39.

*He that believeth on me, as the scripture hath said, out of your belly shall flow rivers of living water. (But this spake he of the Spirit, which they that believe on him should receive: for the Holy Ghost was not yet given; because that Jesus was not yet glorified.*

First John 2:20 says "...ye have an unction from the Holy One..." Understand that this river is in all of us, everyone who is a born-again, spirit-filled believer. God wants to get you to a place where you discipline your life so that the river, or anointing, is continually flowing. Everybody that you touch or come in contact with should be affected. You may not be singing a song or quoting a Scripture — but you bless everyone you come in contact with because of your disciplined life as a worshiper. You allow Him to flow forth through you freely in every situation, in every conversation, in every area of your life.

You may need to go to a bank to get a loan for something. You have been praying about it, and you have been fasting about it. You have been believing God. You go in and sit down and that anointing and that river will begin to flow, and before you know it, before the loan officer can finish asking information, he will say you have got the money. It may be a job or promotion for which you are believing God. You are wondering how you are going to get it because so-and-so is more qualified than you are, but the Scripture says that promotion is of the Lord — and you get it! These very situations have happened in my life. "For promotion cometh neither from the east, nor from the west, nor from the south. But God is the judge: he putteth down one, and setteth up another" (Ps. 75:6,7).

When you recognize the pool of His anointing is inside you and you are living a disciplined life as a worshiper, you can go in confidence. All you have to do is release God's anointing.

This was the miracle of Second Chronicles 20. It was through worship that Jehoshaphat's army was able to prevail. God told them in verse 17 that the battle was not theirs, but His. He told them to simply worship Him. As they followed the Lord's instructions, verse 22 tells us that when they began to sing and praise, the Lord set ambushments against the enemy. They became confused and destroyed each other and all Judah had to do was go in and gather the spoil. They simply released the anointing of God. You don't have to go in under your own might or power and wonder if this thing is going to happen or how it is going to turn out. All you have to do is go in there and say, "God, be God all by Yourself. I have laid my petitions before You. You know my heart." He will do the rest! Remember, the

Word of God says it is the anointing that breaks the yoke of bondage. It was the anointing that drove away the evil spirt from Saul as David played for him. "And it came to pass, when the evil spirit from God was upon Saul, that David took a harp, and played with his hand: so Saul was refreshed, and was well, and the evil spirit departed from him."

As we practice the presence of God, we will also sense the release of His anointing. Often times through our worship, God's anointing is made manifest in the midst of our situations. That is why it is important to continually praise God. Psalm 34 directs us to bless the Lord at *all* times.

*"I will bless the Lord at all times: His praise shall continually be in my mouth. My soul shall make her boast in the Lord: the humble shall hear thereof, and be glad. 0 magnify the Lord with me, and let us exalt His name together. I sought the Lord, and He heard me, and delivered me from all my fears.*

Psalm 34:1-4

We release God's presence as we speak His Name in the earth. You and I are the salt of the earth, the light of the world.

*Ye are the salt of the earth: but if the salt have lost his savor, wherewith shall it be salted? it is thenceforth good for nothing, but to be cast out, and to be trodden under foot of men. Ye are the light of the world. A city that is set on a hill cannot be hid.*

Matthew 5:13-14

Because we are in the world and God's Spirit is in us, it allows God to place us in situations to release His anointing and hold up a standard. We must see ourselves as vessels for God to flow through and then make ourselves available for Him to work through us.

# Chapter VIII

# The Second Flood

**W**hen the streams flow from you and me and from everyone else who understands and begins to live a disciplined life of worship, we will all enter into the presence of God. Everything that I have shared with you thus far is preparation for this chapter. Read it carefully and prayerfully, for I believe that what I am about to share with you is already beginning to happen around our country and in other parts of the world. I believe that praise and worship will be a vital part of what many have said is to be the greatest move of God the world has ever seen. We already see praise and worship crossing denominational lines and beginning to draw the body of Christ together, but there is something even more wonderful that is going to happen. Joel 2:28 says, "I will pour out my Spirit upon *all* flesh." It is my belief that through God's people, united in worship, God's Spirit will flood the earth. When you and I understand what is flowing forth from us, we will experience the vision of Ezekiel 47 as a corporate body. The whole earth will be flooded with God's presence.

> *Afterward he brought me again unto the door of the house; and, behold, waters issued out from under the threshold of the house eastward: for the forefront of the house stood toward the east, and the waters came down from under from the right side of the house, at the south side of the altar. Then brought he me out of the way of the gate northward, and led me about the way without unto the utter gate by the way that looketh eastward; and, behold, there ran out waters on the right side.*
>
> Ezekiel 47:1, 2

I want to show you what the Lord has shown me! One of the things that I began to do when I understood this was to pray, when I meet together with my praise and worship team, and with other ministries, saying, "Lord, I thank you for the river that flows forth from me right now in the Name of Jeus. I combine that with the river that flows forth from my sister, and I combine it with the river that flows from my brother right now in the Name of Jesus. I combine that with the river that flows forth from the musicians, that flows forth from the pastor, that flows forth from the congregation. As I begin to speak that out, in my mind I begin to see it. I see these rivers beginning to come together. I see this big mass of water beginning to come up.

*And when the man that had the line in his hand went forth eastward, he measured a thousand cubits, and he brought me through the waters; the waters were to the ankles.*

Ezekiel 47:3

You see, when we come into worship, and we begin to understand it as disciplined worshipers, all of a sudden we will begin to sense the waters (anointing) beginning to rise up. It will probably start out just ankle deep. There has to be a starting point, but then all of a sudden it will begin to rise.

*Again he measured a thousand, and brought me through the waters; the waters were to the knees...*

Ezekiel 47:4a

The river is beginning to rise. When we begin to unite in corporate worship, the river will begin to rise. When Ezekiel saw it, it was going out through the floor. It was moving out.

*Again he measured a thousand, and brought
me through; the waters were to the loins.*

**Ezekiel 47:4b**

The waters (worship) began to rise more. Do
you see what I am saying here? As we begin to
enter into His presence, the anointing increases.

*Afterward he measured a thousand; and it
was a river that I could not pass over: for
the waters were risen, water to swim in, a
river that could not be passed over.*

**Ezekiel 47:5**

You see, when worship is unhindered, it rises
to a level that is uncontrolled; it flows this way
and that way. It begins to move out over the
earth. When we understand what God wants to
do, saints, what will happen is that through this
level of worship people are going to be affected
everywhere. It will be as if floodgates that have
been closed for many years were suddenly
opened.

*And he said unto me, Son of man, hast thou
seen this? Then he brought me, and caused
me to return to the brink of the river. Now
when I had returned, behold, at the bank of*

*the river were very many trees on the one
side and on the other.*
Ezekiel 47:6, 7

When we begin to move in this capacity we
are going to begin to see the trees and the fruit
manifested on the right side and on the left side
of us, trees giving life and fruit that remains!
They will be manifested because of the river that
is flowing forth, that constant flow of God's
anointing, God's power through the body of
Christ entering into a disciplined life of worship.

*Then said he unto me, These waters issue
out toward the east country, and go down
into the desert and go into the sea [the sea of
mankind] which being brought forth into the
sea, the waters shall be healed.*
Ezekiel 47:8

The healing power of God is going to begin to
move in a dimension we have never seen before
as we begin to release the river, the flood of His
anointing. And because of living the disciplined
life of a worshiper, when we come together, it is
*not* going to take us two or three songs to get in
His presence. We are going to enter into a place
where the anointing of God will begin to rise up
immediately. We are going to feel it at our ankles.

Then, we are going to feel it at our knees. We are going to feel it at our waists, and then it is going to overtake us. Before we know it, people are going to run into our sanctuaries. I believe it with all my heart. They are going to be drawn by the power and the anointing of God. They are not going to understand what it is, but they are going to come in, and their lives are going to be changed.

> *And it shall come to pass, that every thing that liveth, which moveth, whithersoever the rivers shall come, shall live: and there shall be a very great multitude of fish, because these waters shall come thither: for they shall be healed; and every thing shall live whither the river cometh. And it shall come to pass, that the fishers shall stand upon it from Engedi even unto Eneglaim; they shall be a place to spread forth nets; their fish shall be according to their kinds, as the fish of the great sea, exceeding many.*
>
> **Ezekiel 47:9-10**

What is He saying? You will become fishers of men! (Mark 1:17) As it begins to come to pass there will be a great multitude of fish. The fish, the people, are going to be healed as a result of the anointing and the rising of the tide, because of the anointing of the level of worship flowing forth from the Church! This is evangelism — God's way!

When we enter into the life of a disciplined worshiper, we are going to experience what Ezekiel 47 is talking about. Through our worship of the living God, we release His Spirit in the earth today to give hope to the hopeless, healing to the nations, and life to a dying world. God said He would not destroy the earth by water again, but He did not say there would never be another flood! The first flood was natural water, and the end result was death. The second flood is the Holy Spirit, and the end result is life!

*And by the river upon the bank thereof, on this side and on that side, shall grow all trees for meat, whose leaf shall not fade, neither shall the fruit thereof be consumed: it shall bring forth new fruit according to his months, because their waters they issued out of the sanctuary: and the fruit thereof shall be for meat, and the leaf thereof for medicine.*

Ezekiel 47:12

The flood gates are open.

Heirs International Ministries (H.I.M. Inc.) is an end time ministry founded in 1980 by John W. Stevenson. In partnership with Widow's Mite International Ministries the focus of the ministry is to reconcile men unto God and to one another. HIM Inc. is comprised of a team of men and women who minister the word of God and praise and worship in prisons, street meetings, college campuses, and churches.

If you are interested in having this ministry in your area you may reach us by writing to:

H.I.M. Inc.,
1015 E. Main St.
Columbus, Ohio 43205,
or
you can call us at
614-252-0020.

You can order the worship tape "Rivers of Life" that is especially recorded to activate the teachings of this book and lead you into a time of worship and rest in the presence of the Lord. The songs are written, arranged, and produced by John W. Stevenson and performed by a selected worship team.

To order your tape send $7.00 and write to: H.I.M. Inc. 1015 E. Main St. Columbus Ohio 43205. Ask for the tape "Rivers of Life". Please allow 4-6 weeks for delivery.

# ORDER FORM

Return with your check or M.O. to H.I.M. Inc. 1015 E. Main St, Columbus, Ohio 43205

| QTY. | DESCRIPTION | UNIT PRICE | TOT. PRICE |
|------|-------------|------------|------------|
|      |             |            |            |
|      |             | TOTAL DUE  |            |

Name _____

Address _____

City _____ State _____ ZIP _____

Date _____ Phone# _____